AWAKENING

TO PROSPERITY:

Setting Yourself

Up To Live

Dr. Jeremy Lopez

AWAKENING TO PROSPERITY – SETTING YOUR SELF UP TO LIVE
By Dr. Jeremy Lopez
Copyright © 2013 by Jeremy Lopez

Published by Identity Network
P.O. Box 383213
Birmingham, AL 35238
www.identitynetwork.net
United States of America
The author can be contacted at customerservice@identitynetwork.net

Book design by
Treasure Image & Publishing
TreasureImagePublishing.com
248.403.8046

TABLE OF CONTENTS

WHAT DO YOU WANT TO SEE? 5

PROSPERITY VS. POVERTY 9

LET THE DEAD BURY THE DEAD 13

GIVE ATTENTION TO HOPE...19

YOU BECOME WHAT YOU THINK....................................25

AWAKENING PROSPERITY IN OTHERS........................29

PROSPERITY FOLLOWS APPRECIATION........................33

RUNNING YOUR LIFE 37

LAWS OF PROSPERITY 41

PROSPEROUS LIFE HABITS...45

ELIMINATE EMPTY SPACE..47

CULTIVATE PROSPERITY 55

PROSPEROUS RELATIONSHIPS.......................................61

ABOVE ALL THINGS 65

PROSPERITY AND WHOLENESS.....................................67

MAKE IT PROSPER...71

BEARING HEALTHY FRUIT 75

WRITE THE VISION..83

WHY SETTLE FOR LITTLE...87

PROSPEROUS WORDS 91

BIO OF DR. JEREMY LOPEZ: 95

OTHER PRODUCT BY DR. LOPEZ:....................................97

WHAT DO YOU WANT TO SEE?

We hear a lot of talk nowadays about riches and wealth and poverty, prosperity and being poor and being rich; being competitive. Which one is it? I have to work hard to do this. I have to work hard to get that. I want to talk about basically awakening to prosperous living. There's got to be a first step in our awakening and advancement of finally leaving where we have been, and going into the place we would like to go.

The first step you have got to do, is to recognize where you are. You have got to recognize what you are attempting to achieve. You have got to have a goal, a vision.

"Write the vision and make it plain on tablets, that he may run who reads it." Habakkuk. 2:2

Write down something upon paper, but write it down, first of all, in your heart. The Lord instructed us to pray in Matthew 6:10, *"Your kingdom come. Your will be done on earth as it is in heaven."* So, you write the vision first of all in your heart by saying, *"This is an establishment. I'm establishing my heart to say this will be done on earth as it is in heaven."* There is a will of God in the heavens that God wants to bring inside of us. And the neatest thing is that it is already established in us, and it's called the Kingdom of the Living God.

So there is a Kingdom in us that speaks of advancement, success, acknowledging the riches and wealth. Acknowledging a better lifestyle for myself. Acknowledging a better way of living. Acknowledging a better way of experiencing life.

Many of us don't experience life, we let life happen to us. But when I experience life, it means my experiences are things that somehow I reach towards and I press towards and if it does not achieve, if it does not go correctly as planned and there is maybe a little fall, I still learn from my experience and I get up, dust myself off and I try again.

There has got to be a beginning within our lives of prosperity or prosperous living. There must be an advancement in trying to get healed. There has got to be a first step in trying to evolve into what I need to evolve into. Yet the entire time I'm taking the first step to evolve into a new substance, a new life for me, I have to realize that I'm not trying to grab hold of it on the outside and find out who has it or who owns it or who has the patent on that… but it's something that is always ingrained inside of my spirit, and if I reach hard and if I seek inwardly and grab a hold of that which lies within, I'll find something that has always been inside me before the foundations of the world. It is something that is inside of my belly, inside of my spirit and it's been asleep but it's longing to be awakened. It's crying out to say, *"Awaken me. Grab me.*

Look to me. Reach to me. Make me alive again." As we begin to search we realize that's the first step: awakening what lies within.

PROSPERITY VS. POVERTY

Anytime we look at prosperity versus poverty, we must understand that prosperity is not about just money. It is about a lifestyle of not just "having the best," but it is a lifestyle of making sure that you experience, and you reach towards and you grab a hold with integrity the quality of the things of life. See, quality is better than quantity. And quality always speaks of the best. Quality always speaks of true prosperity. Quality of something is the difference between a McDonald's hamburger and a steak at a really nice, (as we say in the south) white table cloth restaurant, that you can experience a juicy big piece of sirloin steak that is cooked to perfection, the way you desire, and seasoned with the things of quality. When you compare the two you see that these are different types of meats. They do not come from the same source. They are not prepared the same. One is a higher type of grade. When we pay attention we recognize these are different, and we say, "Wait a minute. Hold on a minute. I have been eating hamburgers for so long, and yet there is something better out there."

Too often we retreat and say to ourselves, "But I cannot *afford* it. I cannot *afford* the greater things. I cannot *afford* to eat the steak. I cannot *afford* to eat of this top grade. I cannot *afford* it because I have never had the kind of money to do that." And see, you have to realize that when you do that, you have prejudged yourself when you say that you will *never* have the money; you will *never* get your hands on it. Therefore you have established the wrong vision in your heart that you will *never* eat at the finest places because you say, "I cannot *afford* it."

All of a sudden we knock down quality. We knock down the best performance. We knock down everything in life that has the name "quality" to it, "top-grade," "the finer things," "the best of." When we do that, we actually knock down ourselves because all of these things are what we are designed for. It is inside of our DNA before we are ever placed inside of our mother's womb. It is who we are. It is not that we are spoiled people trying to reach for something because we feel like we deserve better. No, it is about knowing and realizing, "This is who I am. And anytime I lower myself from having one of the finer things of quality in my life, I lower my very nature."

> *Grace and peace be multiplied to you in the knowledge*
> *of God and of Jesus our Lord, as His divine power has*
> *given to us **all things that pertain to life and godliness**,*
> *through the knowledge of Him who called us by glory*
> *and virtue, by which have been given to us exceedingly*
> *great and precious promises, that **through these you***
> ***may be partakers of the divine nature**, having escaped*
> *the corruption that is in the world through lust.*
> *2 Peter 1:2-5*

Here Peter mentions being a partaker of Jesus' divine nature, which is divinity, quality, divine perfection, the best quality of Himself.

What is the nature of God?

His nature is this: God doesn't *have* love; He *IS* love. (1 John 4). His nature is that of a King, not a pauper. His nature only understands quality. His nature is "I am perfection." We realize, then that we are part of the Creator. We are part of the universe that God created that is creating in the atmosphere great things.

Why are the great things created? Do you realize, the great things are created for us? Who makes the bad things of life then? Unfortunately, We do. Those bad things were created because we feel that poor quality is the best that we feel we *deserve*. It is what we deserve. "I *deserve* the worst." So what happens is I create for my world the worst. And guess what, My neighbor begins to join in with me and says, 'You know what, I also deserve bad because I am not a good person. I do not deserve good things.' They begin to partake in the bad things I create.

See we are creators and as we stop to realize that, "I'm creating things around me that are bad. I am creating my world, and my world is creating things (not just for me now), but others are taking off of my tree and partaking of this wrong mentality. They are eating from me, and as they eat from me they begin to also feel the same way I do." So we live in a world where we create bad things, and other people join in with it and eat of the bad of ourselves as well.

But God creates good things, He creates prosperous things. He creates great things, and when we begin to grab a hold of that, we begin to understand that God, our Creator, wants us to enjoy the best, the finer, the things of quality with integrity because this is who we are.

LET THE DEAD BURY THE DEAD

*Brethren, I count not myself to have apprehended it, but this one thing I do: **forgetting those things which are behind, and reaching forth unto those things which are before**, I press toward the mark for the prize of the high calling of God in Christ Jesus.*

Philippians 3:13-14

This principle is the same when you renew your mind to prosperity. If you've had past troubles of a financial nature, for example, there's no need to rehearse them. You do not think of them at all. You do not tell people that your parents had poverty all of your life. You do not tell the hardships of your early life and where you are from. Where you are from is not an important issue. It is where you are going that is important.

When I am around people I do not always tell them, "Oh my family had bad things, and I experienced this bad moment in my life. You know, I'm from the ghetto. I'm from the slums. I never had anything." You see, people do not care about where you are from; they care about where you are going. When I am around people, I always ask the question, "So what are you doing?" When we want to find out about people, we ask, "What do you do for a living? Where do you live? What side of town do you live on? Oh great! I like that shirt you have on... where did you get that shirt?"

Those types of questions pull into the present, because people want to know first of all where you stand right now in your life. Knowing where you stand right now in your life will automatically tell me where you are headed.

If I ask someone, "What do you do for a living?" And they say, "Well I am an attorney. I have my own law firm," or "I am actually an entrepreneur, and I am getting into place starting a new business," or maybe "I have a business doing this," or maybe "I am an accountant, or maybe I do this or maybe I do that." By those simple statements, you automatically tell me where you are headed in your future.

But if you tell me things of the past by saying, "Well, you know, it has been hard for me and I never seem to make it on a job. I have been fired ten times. My mom, she was poor, my dad was poor. My dad comes from this side of the tracks, and my mom comes from here." After hearing all of that, I do not want to hang around you anymore because I realize what you are speaking of is not even a present reality. It's dead. It is telling me of something that does not even exist. The past does not exist anymore. There is no such thing as a past. Now, do we have an experience of the past? Yes. But that is the only thing we can take with us: an experience that will carry on into our present.

You can learn from your past experience. Let the dead bury the dead, as Jesus said (Matthew 8:22), and allow the substance of that thing, (that memory, that mindset of that experience), ultimately die, but learn from the experience. When you do that, you take the good out of the bad and begin to apply the good that you've learned at times when you find yourself in a similar situation, and you discover how to get out of those situations. When you can do that, you will find your entire life begins to change.

Therefore if someone asks me right now, "What do you do in your life?" I would answer, "I am slowly advancing into making a career for my life. I am finishing school, I am going through this program, or maybe I am getting some great ideas of things I want to do concerning this or concerning that. Concerning clothing. Concerning jewelry." I am speaking about hope and a future (Jeremiah 29:11). I have planted within the mind of people that, "You know what, this guy is on the road to prosper. He is on the road to movement."

See, everything in life moves and evolves and breaths and shifts. Everything does. Everything God creates is always going to be in movement. There is going to be a life, and there is going to be a death, and in between the life and the death, there is something called movement. It's like flowers that blossom on a tree, and then in the winter they die back. But in the midst of the flowers dying back in the winter, guess what happens? It is already pre-programmed for success. It knows that in the next season, it will produce again. The tree does not say, "Well, you know what, I did not survive last winter. I actually did not make it. My flowers died, so look at me. I am just dried up, there are no leaves on me, I am no longer green, I am no longer pretty. I am just a dried up mess." The tree does not focus on that condition and say, "Well this is who I am and what I am now, so, who knows, next season I project it is going to be the same way."

NO! A tree would never say that, because a tree is designed in such a way that even when it goes through a hard season, or goes through this winter season, and there are things that will be cut back and things that will die, but it is going to be okay because it is created for success and created to bloom again.

You can say within yourself, "There is an awakening in me, that I am getting ready for the next season to begin to produce again." Just like the tree, you can know that even though there is a cut-back, it is not your demise, and you're going to live again.

We have to realize that awakening. The first steps of prosperity is realizing that, even through hard times, it is not a big deal. Through your experience, you learn, "this too shall pass." These temporal circumstances are subject to change. Learn to take the good from the bad because people want to hear good news. People want to know, "So, what do you currently doing? What are you involved with? What side of town do you live on?" And they begin a conversation with you. Men start a conversation with each other with, "What team are you rooting for? How are the Braves doing this year in baseball?" or something like that. They typically don't answer with, "Well you know, I just, um... I do not know. I am not a baseball fan because, you know, none of them ever win." Or, "they are all going to go downhill." No! Rather they'll say, "You know, this year my team did not do too good, but next year they will be better."

Hope is defined as a **confident expectation of good**. We were created to hope, and to expect the good. It is in your DNA to always look and say, "I see what is going on, but it is going to get better." Hebrews 6:19 tells us that hope is an anchor for our soul. People instinctively want to tell the good news. You get excited about the good news. People rejoice with good news.

The first stages to your prosperity is to learn through the bad, and to speak of only the good because you are programmed for success. You begin to say, "Let the dead bury the dead. It is over with." Put poverty and all things that pertain to poverty completely behind you and forget them. You have to accept a certain theory of the universe as being correct, and resting all of your hopes and happiness in it being correct.

GIVE ATTENTION TO HOPE

What can you gain by giving heed to conflicting theories? For example, if you are reading books about the world coming to an end, or how bad people are saying it is, put them aside. Those are bad books for you. They are not feeding your hope. You do not need to read books about, "Oh things are looking bad. We have a bad president in the Oval Office, and the world is going to come to an end." If you feed on kind of expectation for disaster, it will kill your dreams. You kill your hopes about your future.

"For I know the plans I have for you," declares the Lord,
"plans to prosper you and not to harm you, plans to give
you hope and a future."
Jeremiah 29:11 (NIV)

God promises that there is a bright future and there is hope. However, once you begin to lose you hope, your future begins to darken and slowly die because you are starving it. The bible tells us that hope deferred makes your heart sick. (Proverbs 13:12). You have to feed your future with hope, just like you would feed your baby. You have to feed your future desires, passions, love, dreams, by beginning to ponder them, think about them, and meditate upon them. When you do that, your perspective changes, and begin to turn what looks like poverty into hope. It looks like it is getting bad, but you begin to turn the pages with hope. You begin to make a paradigm shift and begin to make it prosperous.

In the Bible, the Lord instructed Joshua,

> *This book of the law shall not depart from your mouth,*
> *but you shall meditate on it day and night...* ***for then***
> ***you will make your way prosperous, and then you will***
> ***have success.*** *Joshua 1:8*

It is obvious from this passage that what you give your attention to and meditate on directly affects your prosperity and success. When you lay hold of hope for your future, or for your prosperity you give life to it, but when you do not give life to your desire, you make it poverty stricken. When you begin to feed life into a dream of the future, and you being to feed passion into it, you begin to create for yourself a world of divine prosperity.

Prosperity means an "overflow; an abundance of; life." Poverty results in death. When you begin to say, "This hobby will never happen for me. It will never be a career for me. It will never make me money. I am going to lose my job any day now." When you look at your life and you say, "I am never going to get a raise. This is no good. I will never make a shift to a new job." Then guess what? You are speaking and proclaiming to yourself poverty. You are not feeding life into a desire in you that says, "There is hope and a bright future. There is something better on the horizon."

I encourage people not to read books concerning some evil end-time or things that feed fear instead of hope. You do not do that. Instead, read about hope and a bright future. Read about the success and the career and the DNA of God in you.

Even Jesus says, *"The words that I speak unto you, they are spirit, and they are life." (John 6:63)*. In the same way, you are called to speak words that are spirit and life into yourself and into your atmosphere. Speak spirit and life into your dreams, your visions and to the reality. Say, "I will only move in the advancement of spirit and I will only move in the advancement of life."

Have hope for a bright future. Your future and life is not going to the devil, and is not getting worse. Although, the world might be getting darker, but that doesn't dictate your future.

*Arise, shine; For your light has come! And the glory of the LORD is risen upon you. For behold, the darkness shall cover the earth, And deep darkness the people; **But the LORD will arise over you, And His glory will be seen upon you.** Isaiah 60:1-2*

What is your world about? What is your atmosphere about? My world is about hope and a bright, glorious future. My world is about prosperity. My world is about abundance. My world is about an overflow, and if I keep the overflow and the goodness of long life ahead of me, that will be prosperous, (again prosperity can be about money or not about money; either way I have a bright future ahead of me). I have dreams that I have not fulfilled yet. I have hopes of things that will begin to shift. Why? Not because I am just hoping for it, but I begin to put my hand involved in it and I begin to plow up the ground of poverty and turn it into prosperity.

Ultimately, how my life will turn out will be a result of what I have thought. Begin to think, "I have the power to turn it around, and make a change no matter what I am having to deal with. Whatever I have to face, I am going to face it and begin to shift and cause a new evolution to happen. I can change what used to be bad and turn it into good. I will make this shift in my life and say 'I am not just going places, I am in those places now. I am already on the journey.'"

The moment you agree with the hope that is inside you already, and believe that, "I am that I am. I am prosperous. My life is amazing." The moment you think that thought, right then and there, you enter into the power of "now" and say, "I already am that thing." It is not about becoming. It is not about some day one day reaching that end result. It is not about having to do this and that to become that thing. The thought in my brain begins to be planted, I begin to acknowledge it, and all of a sudden I become that at the present moment.

When Jesus used the words, "The words that I speak are spirit and life," the word "spirit" in the Greek literally means "*now.*" Therefore it says, "The words I speak are about the nowness, the present reality of the life you live." In other words, I am here to give you life and give it to you more abundantly. It is not about a futuristic thing, but It is about, "think it now, and you will already be it."

See if I am thinking it now, I am not *becoming* it, I *am* already it. I want to live in the reality that I am already prosperous and the past is done away with. It is over with. I am not going to bring up the past. I am not going to plow the ground that is already dead. I am going to plow a new ground, new territory and begin to project, believe and know that in my nowness it already has manifested.

YOU BECOME WHAT YOU THINK

Why give time and attention to things which are being removed through the evolutionary part of your growth when you can basically hasten the removal only by promoting the evolution growth of what you need to be thinking now and move into it? Go ahead and go for it. You have to realize right now there is an evolutionary growth in your life that is saying "which way do you want me to go?" What are you evolving into? Your life is nothing but about movement. So you are going to be moving. You are going to be moving in whatever direction you need to be moving in. And if you think for a moment you are staying still, you are never sitting still. You are always evolving into something, and whatever you are going to evolve into is going to be a result of what you have previously one second, two seconds, a millisecond, thought about.

*For as a man **thinks in his heart**, so is he.*
Proverbs 23:7

Whatever I am thinking about this moment is what I am in movement towards. The evolution in my spirit begins to say, "I am going to evolve into that thought. I am evolving into that. There is growth in that thought. There is growth in that evolution so let's go for it." It begins to promote it, it begins to speak in my body, "This is the direction we are going. I am steering the ship. This is the season for us to move into it." And what does it need? What does it ask for? It asks for a thought. It asks for a piece of the puzzle right there, and every piece that I feed it, it begins to run after that.

Furthermore, brethren, whatsoever things are true, whatsoever things are honest, whatsoever things are just, whatsoever things are pure, whatsoever things are worthy love, whatsoever things are of good report, if there be any virtue, or if there be any praise, **think on these things.** *Philippians 4:8*

So, whatever you do, give your attention entirely to riches. Ignore poverty. Whenever you think or speak of those who are poor, think and speak of them as those who are becoming rich. As those who are here to move into that area. Do not look at their situation and say, "Well they are poor now." No, move into that area to say, "They are prospering. They are prospering now." It is not all about you, it is about other people. Think the thoughts of goodness towards others. Think the thoughts of riches towards others, then they and others will catch the inspiration and begin to search for the way out of it.

You do not come into agreement with the current stages people are in; rather, you speak into their *nowness* and change the paradigm shift of their thought in the now to say, "Hey, you know what? You are on a new path now. Hey, here is a new thought for you."

What do we mean when we say, "Here is food for thought." When I say, "Here is food for thought" instantly what I am saying is, "I am going to replace the thought you just had with a brand new thought. So, here is food for your new thoughts." The shift comes and replaces the mindset of poverty with a mindset of prosperity. It starts an evolution, a Genesis effect, of the beginning stages of awakening to that reality of who you have always been. You move into that realm.

No matter how horrible the conditions may seem in your country, your state, your business, your life, your career, you don't consider those things. Do not waste your time. Do not destroy your hope by considering or giving thought to how 'horrible' the natural circumstances may be. Instead, consider that, "My DNA is already programmed and created for great things, great quality, etc." Keep a confident expectation of good and prosperity.

Do not think about anything that will not take you to great and greater. It is not worth it. When you consider a thought, answer this question, "Will this thought take me to something great, and then take me to something greater?" If it does not, do not give into it. It is not worth it. Because if you give into a thought, and that thought is known to get worse and 'worser,' then you are going to end up in the worst state of your life. You might say, "I did not ask for this." And your spirit is going to say, "Yes, actually you did. Because you thought something that you knew would spiral down to get worse, and then (the ultimate of the worse), 'worser.'

AWAKENING
PROSPERITY IN OTHERS

You have to remember that you become what you think about. You must change your perspective to see people considered poor as people who are becoming rich; see them as those who are to be congratulated rather than pitied. When your perspective changes to see them as they are, you address them differently, and it lifts them out of a state of poverty.

When you say, "Congratulations where you are right now." And they might say, "Are you crazy? Do you see what is going on in my life? Do you recognize how bad it is?" You can say, "Actually, I do not. I do not give recognition to the bad. I am not going to pity you for where you are, **because I know that there is joy that comes in the morning**. I know that things are going to get better."

*Let no foul or polluting language, nor evil word nor unwholesome or worthless talk [ever] come out of your mouth, **but only such [speech] as is good and beneficial to the spiritual progress of others**, as is fitting to the need and the occasion, **that it may be a blessing and give grace (God's favor) to those who hear it.***
Ephesians 4:29 (AMP)

I know it is going to get better because when you consider thoughts of increase and blessing, instantly at that present moment you begin to increase. So, rather than pity people, it is more fitting to congratulate them and say, "Wow, things are looking up for you. You may not see it but I see it."

What you want to do is bring their mind into an alignment with the good thoughts you are thinking about them, and for them and towards them. As you begin to think and say, "Congratulations on what you have accomplished." And they look and they say, "What have I accomplished? Are you crazy? Do you know where I live? Do you know what I own? Do you know what I have?" And I say, "Absolutely. Congratulations." Their mindset may have been focused on what they feel they were lacking, "Don't you know that I have an old car? Do you understand I live in a one-room apartment?" but you speak words that remind them of their accomplishments...

"Yes! At one point you did not have a car. Congratulations. There is promotion. Congratulations! You know where you are is better than where you used to be." And you begin to congratulate people where they are so where they will make a paradigm shift in their brain so they will begin to recognize the blessing that is in their life now, and have expectation for it to increase. Your words interrupt the downward spiral of their poverty thoughts of, "It is bad, I only have a little bit." You cause them to rethink and evolve into a new lifestyle of think to begin to say, "It is better. I used to live with my parents, now I have my own apartment. It might be one room, but congratulations to myself. I used to not have a car. I used to have a bicycle, now I have maybe an old beat-up car. Congratulations, I have moved somewhere." They can then recognize prosperity in their life. This also fosters and feeds a heart of gratitude.

Your life is always going to be in movement. Pay attention to where you came from, and you will to move in a state of gratification and gratitude. You find an inward peace that says, "You know what, I am happy with what I have." And all of a sudden you move away from where you came from when you did not have anything to a state of being of, "Wow, now I have recognized the movement in my life moving me to a place of now. I do have substance of something."

PROSPERITY FOLLOWS
APPRECIATION

Life is not about looking at things and saying, "This is bad. This is good." When you look in comparison, anything can look bad or good. A one-room apartment is bad when you compare it to a mansion. It is not bad at all. Mansions are not good. People who have mansions have a lot of money they have to dish out every month for mortgages, unless they are very rich and they already own it. And even if they are filthy rich to already own it, they still have property taxes, they still have light bills, they still have things that you are not even aware of because you are not in their shoes. You are not in their atmosphere.

So you have to look at life to realize that what you have might be small, but it does not make it bad. It only becomes bad when you empower it with a thought that says "You are bad," and when you define it as being "bad." When you define it as being "bad," then to you it is bad.

But to someone else who has the exact same thing you have, because they come from a state of thankfulness and gratefulness and they begin to enjoy what they have, then for them it is a good thing. And guess who gets promoted? Not you, they do.

Because they appreciate. They see the ladder of the movement moving them higher and greater and they know, "Hey, you know what? I am moving into divine prosperity. I am moving into prosperity because I used to live with my parents, now I have a one-room apartment. I am moving into divine prosperity." The shift begins to take place, and their mind focuses on being thankful for the prosperity, that is not necessarily *coming to* them, but the prosperity they *currently hold*. Then, because they are grateful and they recognize "I am prosperous," then now prosperity automatically begins to connect them. The frequency of prosperity in the universe that God initiated, which is, "Think upon this and you will begin to have it. Think upon these things, and it will become yours."

*And Jesus answering saith to them, `**Have faith of God**;*
for verily I say to you, that whoever may say to this
mount, Be taken up, and be cast into the sea, and may
not doubt in his heart, but may believe that the things
*that he saith do come to pass, **it shall be to him***
***whatever he may say.** Mark 11:22-23 (YLT)*

You will have what you think and speak. You may wonder, "Wow, prosperity keeps on coming to me. Why is it that favor and prosperity keep on coming to me?" It is because you have already thought yourself to be wealthy. You have already thought yourself to be prosperous. You have already recognized your life to be great and prosperous and happy and joyful, and prosperity says, "You have appreciated me, so congratulations! Here is more of me to you." And it begins to wrap itself up to you as a gift because you already have divine prosperity. You already have a part of prosperity when you recognize and are grateful for what you have now. You recognize the good and the prosperity in your life now, and your life begins to say, "Congratulations, I am going to give you more of what you are grateful for."

When your mind is renewed to prosperity, you begin to recognize prosperity in others as well. When you see the poor, or those who the world calls "less fortunate," you begin to look at them as prospering and say, "I am not going to say 'poor thing.' I am going to congratulate you, because you are moving up. Even if you do not see it, my mind thinks prosperity for you." Their mind may think poverty, and compares with others and says, "I do not have what you have." But the prosperous mind does not make those kind of comparisons.

Levels of prosperity are never about comparison to other people. Once you compare the levels of other people, you automatically welcome poverty and discomfort and disease (dis-ease) into your life because you set your mind to the life of comparison. When you do that, you step into the vicious cycle of trying to keep up with the Jones', which will always keep you dissatisfied. It keeps you in a mentality of lack. It keeps you at a place where you are never going to be happy. My level will never be your level, and your level will never be my level, and I do not want it to be. I do not desire your level. I want my level.

When you realize, "I am prosperous now. I am wealthy beyond measure of what I can currently see in my life," then you begin to welcome that wealth and prosperity, and your life begins to change. It causes a shift of the universe that says, "Congratulations, welcome to the next level of your life."

RUNNING YOUR LIFE

I remember back in my life, for many many years, *(and basically it was because of ignorance)*, I had allowed life to run me, as opposed to me running it. Like many of us, I was not really taught how to prosper. We are just human beings trying to get by, trying to survive, and not really taught that we actually are leaders, and co-creators in God with authority to be able to run life.

After studying many teaching CDs, books, and different things that I have paid attention to, something in me began to awaken to realize that in this life, you have got to learn to take the reigns of the horse called "life." You have to run it.

How do you run it? You run it by your thoughts. You run it by what you speak. Understand that thoughts become things. What you perceive, sense, and establish within your heart through your thinking process, will produce the reality of those things. It will produce what you desire, want, visualize and think.

Is life about wishful thinking? No. It is about establishing a foundation deep in your heart of having an assurance of what you are looking for, what you desire and what you want.

*Now **faith is the assurance** (the confirmation, the title
deed) of the things [we] hope for, being the **proof of
things [we] do not see** and the **conviction of their
reality** [faith perceiving as real fact what is not revealed
to the senses].* Hebrews 11:1

I always tell people to devise a plan; get a strategy in the Kingdom of God for what you know God wants for you as an individual. It is not about what other people desire, what other people have, or what other people want. There are always going to be the "Joneses," that you will be tempted to keep up with, but you are going to have to learn to find your <u>own</u> identity. Come to the place of awakening in your spirit to know who you are, what you are, what you are called to be, and what you are called to have for you as an individual as opposed to what everyone else seems to have.

Often, people tend to ride out the waves of what "everybody else" has. Because of that, they are inclined to lose their identity and who they are. If you do this, you actually lose in the mix of life of what <u>you </u>truly desire as well as what you <u>need </u>in you life. If you do not know yourself and your identity, then what someone else needs in their life, you will be wanting the need of what they have. No wonder there are so many people dissatisfied.

If you begin to take on the need of someone else, then it is not going to be possible for you to discover who you are and discover your own desires. What happens is, you lose your identity and also lose what you want, and need for your life.

What someone else has is not always the answer for you. I found myself at a place, *(once again, through good teachings and books)*, that I had to learn that it was not about riding off the waves of other people and what they had. It was not about trying to keep up with the Joneses. Nor was it about "wishful thinking," or moving into this thought process of knowing that if I just think it I am going to just have anything I desire in my life. But rather, you have to realize the universe, or God, Jesus, they are not Santa Claus. They are not this jeanie. The Bible says, *"God is a Spirit: and they that worship him must worship him in spirit and in truth.."* (John 4:24)

There has got to be a sense of reverence, a sense of holiness, and a sense of passion to want to be able to seek God, and ask God what He desires for you as an individual to have. The bottom line is everyone of us are *"fearfully and wonderfully made."* (Psalm 139:14). We are all unique. We all have different DNAs. We all have different thumbprints. Therefore, what works for another, might not work for me.

LAWS OF PROSPERITY

When we are dealing with the laws of prosperity, we are first of all dealing with how to set yourself up to finding who you are, what you are, what **you** need for **you** in **your** life that will work for you, and then get the definition and the revelation of what prosperity is and means to **you**. (Because, once again, prosperity is going to be different across the board for other people.)

We know prosperity basically means "an abundance of." When you begin to understand the terminologies and the definitions of true prosperity, you will find that prosperity is a mental thing, prosperity is a soulish thing, prosperity is a spiritual thing, and prosperity is a natural thing.

You can have all the money in the world, and yet have your soulish man or your spirit man be broke as ever. If your mind is not prospering to the level that it needs to prosper, then no matter how much gold, riches and wealth you have on the outside, you will not be prosperous and you will still be miserable.

Those who are truly blessed with the bliss and the joy of life are those who know they are prospering on the inside; knowing their identity, having an assurance and a foundation of who they are. These people know their limitations, they know their boundaries of what they need, what they do not need. They know what makes them empowered and what does not make them empowered.

Money does not make you empowered if you are fragmented in your heart. If your are fragmented in the soulish man, then money will never heal that. Poverty in the soulish realm takes something else to be able to heal and satisfy it. It takes getting to the root problem in the soul. Money is not the answer for your soulish man. Money is not the answer for your spirit man.

But in the natural realm, the Bible says, *"Money answers all things." (Ecclesiastes 10:19)*. Money is the key, or the answer, to the natural function and flow of the patterns of society because money tends to answer and buy and purchase and trade, and provides whatever you need in this natural realm. Therefore money only answers this natural realm, but is not the answer for the soulish man or the spirit man.

In order to understand your identity, you need to have the *"Ah-hah"* moment, or the revelation in the soulish realm and in the spirit realm to know who you are and who your soulish man is. You need to know your mind, your will, and emotions: what they do, their functionality, and how they can bless you. You need to understand the power that soulish realm possesses, and understanding it to the degree that you can define it, you can control it, and it works for you, and you do not work for it.

If you work for the soulish man, that means your emotions will run you crazy. You will get mad, you will get angry, you will be jealous, you will be deceitful, and you will be dishonest. All of those emotions would run you. Once you get hold of your soulish man, you will identify with its power and what it can do for you, and through you. You will discover ownership over it, then you begin to control your mind, will and emotions. This will help you direct it in the way it needs to be directed.

It's also the same way spiritually. You begin to set up who God is over you in your spirit, and who does and does not run your life, and what control you have.

> *And, behold, a woman, which was diseased with an issue of blood twelve years, came behind him, and touched the hem of his garment:* **for she said within herself, "If I may but touch his garment, I shall be whole."** *But Jesus turned him about, and when he saw her, he said, "Daughter, be of good comfort; thy faith hath made thee whole." And the woman was made whole from that hour.* Matthew 9:20-22

From this scripture, we see an account of a woman who had the issue of blood. She had a disease which caused on her menstrual cycle to last for twelve years, and therefore she was bleeding profusely. She came to Jesus and when she did, the Bible says that she said **"within herself."** She had to push through the crowd, but the Bible says, *"She said within herself, if I can just reach up and touch His garment, I will be healed."*

There came an agreement inside of herself and within of her spirit, inside of her mental consciousness as well that *"I know the foundation of agreement says inside of me that if I reach up and touch Him, I am going to be automatically healed."*

There has to be that agreement inside of you, that faith, that **assurance** to know who you are, what you are, and your limitations and what you can do inside of you. When you bring that all into the power of agreement, then you are learning how to prosper more because you have a control over that thing and not letting it run you.

PROSPEROUS LIFE HABITS

When we are discussing prosperity, we are talking about how to set you up and prepare you to be able to move in the overflow, move in the realm to prosper in <u>any</u> and <u>every</u> level of your life.

The first stage in setting yourself up to prosper is you have to learn to **create a vacuum to receive.** What I mean is that you have to be able to, first and foremost, rid your life of all the junk, all the empty space that you have within your mind, body, your affairs and your relationships. This affects everything in your life. You have to create a vacuum to suck out everything that does not need to be there including heavy weights, burdens, negative thinking, wrong thinking, and wrong interactions with people. There are so many things we accumulate in every area of our lives that basically causes us to be poverty-stricken.

For example, you can be in a wrong relationship and that wrong relationship be as poverty to you, versus adding to your life and making you prosperous. Anytime someone is adding to your life, multiplying your life, empowering your life, then that person is prosperity to you. You can then begin to receive and exchange of prosperity with them.

*The generous man will be prosperous, **And he who waters will himself be watered.** Proverbs 11:25*
*Blessed be the God and Father of our Lord Jesus Christ, the Father of mercies and God of all comfort, who comforts us in all our affliction, **so that we may be able to comfort those who are in any affliction, with the comfort with which we ourselves are comforted** by God. 2 Corinthians 1:3-4*

When you know who you are and your identity, then you are able to lift other people, encourage them, exhort them, comfort them, and feed into them, that substance that will cause them to take on that load of prosperity by what you have fed into them, and given them for the rest of their lives, and they will do the same for you. If you know how to empower somebody and someone knows how to empower you, then you have a prosperous relationship. You have a prosperous friendship.

ELIMINATE EMPTY SPACE

You have to create a vacuum get rid of empty space. **What is empty space?**

*In the beginning God created the heavens and the earth. The earth was **without form**, and **void**; and **darkness** was on the face of the deep... Genesis 1:1-2*

We can see from this passage that the earth is a picture of what "empty space" is. The earth was formless. It was void. It was chaotic because it lacked knowledge; it was "ignorant." Darkness is a type of ignorance. There was no prosperity, there was no addition, there was no multiplication, there was no productivity. In that moment, there was no movement involved to take the earth to a higher state of consciousness or a higher state of being. The earth was without form. It was not prospering. There was no grass turning green. There was no life. There was no productivity. There was no fruit. There were no trees. There were no valleys. There was nothing that was a constant cycle that moved to a place of productivity. Therefore, the earth was ignorant.

Empty space in your life and consciousness are areas of ignorance. Ignorance is a place void of light and substance. You have to examine your life; if your life has empty space, then you are moving into a place of ignorance or darkness.

Darkness **exists** when you cannot see your hand before your face. It is a lack of awareness. It is when you do not know where you are, what you are involved with, or what is around you, how close you are to an obstacle, or how close you are to victory. You do not know how close you are to something evil, something good, a pitfall or a stepping-stone. You have no clue because you are walking in darkness. You are walking without vision. You are walking in ignorance.

When you hear someone who says, *"So-and-so is in darkness,"* what he or she is saying is this person is actually in ignorance. They do not know what is around them.

This is the **reality** for many people on planet earth: that many of us are literally on the verge of a total breakthrough, but because we suffer from a lack of knowledge. The Bible says, *"My people are destroyed for lack of knowledge."* (Hosea 4:6) Too often, we suffer because we do not know what we possess, and we do not know who we are.

We can be on the verge of a divine breakthrough but not enter in because we are unaware of it. We do not recognize it.

Many people are literally one step away from becoming multi-millionaires. People all around the globe are one step away from an invention that will make them billionaires. People are one step away from creating a thought that can take their lives to a whole different dimension, and never look back again to suffering, to poverty, to lack, to depression, to rejection, to rebellion. We are all one-step away. Therefore, we suffer from a lack of knowledge because that one step between that one step and us is a place called "ignorance," or a darkness or empty space or void or formlessness.

*The earth was **without form**, and **void**; and **darkness** was on the face of the deep. And the Spirit of God was hovering over the face of the waters. Then God said, "**Let there be light**"; and there was light. Genesis 1:2-3*

When we look at that, we have to realize that the earth was ignorant, and dark. Then God called for light. You have to create a vacuum to suck out all the ignorance, darkness and all the empty spaces in your life. It does not mean you have to clutter your mind full of things and ideas, but it means you need to fill your mind full of light; full of productive, prosperous teachings, prosperous music, and prosperous conversations.

Anything that goes into your ear needs to be full of prosperous things that bring light to your mind, where your mind is always turning over with fresh and new creative ideas. That way you will be able realize that you are a conduit of prosperous living because prosperous things are always flooding into your spirit, into my mind, and into my subconscious.

Here is the problem with most people: the reason their soulish man does not prosper is because that are feeding into their ears and eyes things that are not productive, things that are not fruitful, things that are not going to grow and multiply.

Many people feed things to their ears that are only for the "now" moment. There's instant gratification, but it has no substance, no root system, and has nothing that has a string of DNA in it that causes it to grow and multiply from good to better, to improvements, to productivity, nor to growth. When we feed ourselves things of the "now" moment, but have no growth potential or string of DNA, then what we feed on goes in and it dies. Then we are left, once again, with a void.

The mind of our hearts begin to receive and consume things that have no life-giving substance to them. Then we wonder why we do not know where we are going, we do not know what we are called to do, and we are constantly thinking thoughts of ignorance; Ignorance, lack, stupidity, full of nothingness, not knowing what to do. "Who is this? Why are they in my life?" All of these questions are ignorance or lack of knowledge. Because of that, we are putting that out in the universe, out in creation, back out to God.

Ignorance may seem like a harsh word, but yet it is not a harsh word. When someone says you are ignorant, it does not mean they are cussing you out. It means you have a lack or a void there of knowledge. You have a lack of wisdom. Therefore what they are saying is that you have to fill the void. What they seeing is your void. When you have these empty spaces of ignorance, then people see more of your emptiness and the empty spaces than they see who you really are. They see closets that are not full of productive things, when they open up those closet doors within your mind or through the conversations you have with them, or through your lifestyle, they perceive more your emptiness than your productivity. Those empty rooms could be filled rooms of divine wisdom that has enough empowerment that would actually last you for days, weeks, months, and years.

*If any of you lacks wisdom, **let him ask of God,** who*
*gives to all **liberally** and without reproach, and it **will** be*
given to him. James 1:5

When you are ignorant, you have a lack of prosperity mentally, socially, physically, and spiritually. You do not have enough energy in you. You do not have enough substance. You do not have enough power of principles in you; whatever is in you won't sustain you more than this moment.

Have you ever been around people who are constantly hungry? All day long they are constantly, hungry, hungry, hungry. "I need more food, I need more substance." Why? Often, if you look at their life, you will find out they are filling their life full of junk food, (potato chips and candy bars, etc.), and full of things that are not feeding them the right nutrition and vitamins and minerals that their body lacks and their body desperately needs. If you constantly eat junk food all day long your will body say, "I have a lack, and what you are feeding me is not fulfilling my need and my desire and the energy that I need to keep this body going throughout the day." You'll constantly eat and eat and eat and never be satisfied. You need nutritional foods to really satisfy hunger.

It's not just unhealthy foods. I am a big salad eater. I love salads because some of the things you can put in salad can be nutritious. But, it all depends on what you put on the salad. If you eat just the lettuce, for example, lettuce itself has no nutritional value. Therefore, it is not going to fill you up completely. You can eat lettuce all day long and by the end of the day, you are starving, shaking because you either have low blood sugar at that moment because your body is saying, "I desperately need substance. Something that has value to it. Vitamins, minerals or something that has a substance to it that is solid that will be able to empower and take care of this body and give it the energy it needs." Take a look at your life. Many of us are not prospering in how we eat.

In the same way, many of us are not prospering spiritually, emotionally and bodily because of the fact that we do not know what to feed ourselves. You have to look at your life and say, "I have got to create a vacuum to suck out everything that is harmful to me, that is toxic to me, things that are not doing to me any value."

To put it another way, you have to release yourself, (your body, your life mentally, socially, spiritually, etc.), and suck those things out that have no nutritional value, that are not producing, not "bearing fruit" (as the Bible says). Rid yourself of what is not bringing full prosperity.

CULTIVATE PROSPERITY

Once you have vacuumed all the junk out and the empty space of your mind, your body, your affairs and your relationships, once you have sucked it all out, then it's time to create a vacuum to _receive_. You have do be a conduit, or a vacuum, to receive all that is pure, good, nutritious, full of value, full of love, full of hope, and full of life.

> _Finally, brethren, whatsoever things are true, whatsoever things are honest, whatsoever things are just, whatsoever things are pure, whatsoever things are lovely, whatsoever things are of good report; if there be any virtue, and if there be any praise, **think on these things**. Philippians 4:8_

That is what God wants for you. God wants to be able to fill your life full of substance, value, integrity and character. Whatever it is in your life that you are lacking, God has the answer that can cause you to never thirst again. Which means, that if you fill your life full of constant integrity and value, and things that are spiritually and physically nutritious for you and adds value to you, that will multiply in you, then you are prospering because of the fact that you have something that will last and **sustain** you; something that will energize you and keep you going for many years to come.

If you think about it, even naturally within your body, if you do not fill your body full of the minerals and the substances that it needs then what happens is your body will get off-balance. You will find yourself in a place where you will get sick, you will get infections easier, you will constantly be trying to find what is wrong with you, you will be lethargic, you will want to sleep all the time, you will lay around all the time. You will become overweight, and you will become very lazy because your body is saying, "I desperately need prosperity. I desperately need substance to feed me so I can be able to be rejuvenated and function and flow the way I should." When your body is lacking in prosperity, then your body becomes fragmented.

This applies in any area of life. Financially, *(money that pays your bills)*: anytime that you are not prospering, you are fragmented. Any area of your life that you are not whole and complete by prospering mentally, spiritually, physically, and socially you are fragmented. That means you are not whole and complete in that specific or particular arena of your life.

You want to set yourself up to be a receiver, to receive only the things that have the power to sustain you and that has the power to multiply. Those things that have the power to bear forth character, integrity, and much much more of itself.

Money has the power and the potential to either leave your hands and you have a minus or depletion, or it has the potential and the power to actually multiply itself. It all depends on how you think.

Do you have a lack of knowledge to know how to make an investment? See, money is your friend, and if money is your friend you have to know that you have the power. You could have the definition, and have the knowledge, and knowledge is great, but knowledge itself is not power. It is knowledge *put to the test*; it is knowledge *put into action* - that is what is powerful. When you have knowledge put into action then you have **revelation**. Then you have a movement. Then you have the reality behind the action beginning to produce and manifest in your life.

You have to know how to take money, and *(not through ignorance, but through knowledge)* put action behind the knowledge to know how to multiply it. Money can multiply. Anything in life will multiply if you know the definition, and if you are empowered to know how to multiply it. If you do not know the wisdom it takes to cause anything in creation to multiply, then you will find it automatically subtracting from your life. You will not even have to do anything. By default it will subtract from your life.

For example, if you do not know how to multiply money, then money will be taken from you. It will not just sit dormant. Many people think that, *"If my money is in my checking account it will just sit dormant. No matter how dumb I am, no matter how much I do not know about how to invest money, the money will still sit there."* This is not true. If you pay attention you'll see that banks will often take out a certain percentage of that money through service fees, and other areas that are not obviously seen. Because of that, your money that you think is sitting dormant is actually decreasing.

Money never sits still. It is like energy, and has to flow. If you lack knowledge on money and you think, "If I just hold my money, it will not go anywhere," that is not true. That is a false belief. A false doctrine, as I call it. Money will flow. It will either flow to produce for you, or money will go, whether you are conscious of it or not. Money will leave your hands very quickly if you do not know how to multiply it, and to invest it. Always, always, always have your money circulating. Always. Have your money circulating so that it will be like energy and flow and will produce for you. Even a little bit of productivity and a little bit more increase is better than no increase at all. Always remember that. I would rather have a little bit than have none. If I don't keep it actively producing, then it will by default move away and subtract from me.

Always remember, be the vacuum. First of all, remove or "suck out" everything in your life that does not need to be there. Secondly, be the vacuum to receive, and draw the things you need in your life.

Be an attractor that causes what you need (the more money, the more knowledge, etc.) to be drawn into your life. The more wisdom you can add to your knowledge, then you will begin to attract more of what you are pondering on, thinking on, and more of what you have the knowledge for. Any area in your life where you are prospering in knowledge, you will automatically begin to prosper in the substance of that area. Conversely, any area of poverty in your soul will not prosper but will subtract.

*Beloved, I wish above all things that you may prosper and be in health, even as **your soul prospers**. 3 John 1:2*

PROSPEROUS RELATIONSHIPS

Now that we have that settled, we have to also look at the different levels concerning relationships.

You have to let go of unpleasant relationships. That is another key to setting yourself up for prosperity. If you are going to prosper, I am going to tell you right now, get rid of those who say they are your friends but are not friendly people. Get rid of those in your life who are just stagnant, who are not really producing anything for you. If someone is not adding to your life, every time you get with him or her, every time you talk to him or her on the phone, you can love him or her from a distance, but you are going to have to walk away from him or her.

Now this doesn't mean that you say, "You are not producing for me. I have to leave you right now." No! You do not want to cause tension. That is not going to draw anything back to you in the universe. God will never bless you for that. Instead, what you have to do is set yourself up to make sure you are a blessing to them, you love them, but you have to slowly gradually walk away from them. The bottom line is, if they are not empowering you, they are taking from you. There is no middle ground here.

Whoever walks with the wise becomes wise, but the companion of fools will suffer harm. Proverbs 13:20

When it comes to relationships, a relationship is once again like money, it has to flow. Relationships will either **regress** or progress. If I have a friend, for example, and I say, "I am not going to talk to you for three years starting today. I will call you in three years." Do you think the relationship is going to lie dormant, or stay stagnant? No, because our lives and lifestyle will never sit still. I am not going to sit in a chair for three years and not eat, not go to the restroom, not grow, not lose my hair, not sleep because I have to go on with life. My body is not set to stay still.

Therefore, when you look at your life and you look at another person's life there is, once again, constant movement. You have a three-year span where there will be constant movement, there will be aging, there will be a new level of learning, there will be a new level of walking away from things, there will be a new level of advancement of what true friends are, what money is, what rejection is, what failure is. You will go through life for three years. You cannot expect three years later to call and say, "Hey, what's up? Everything is back to the way it used to be." It will not happen. Life just does not stay still. You cannot expect a relationship to stay still. It is either going backwards or it is going to take you forwards.

You need to examine every relationship you have. If a relationship is not empowering you, if it is not feeding into you,

and you have to be a blessing back. You cannot expect to be blessed without being a blessing back. Everything in the earth flows and functions this way.

"While the earth remains, seedtime and harvest, cold and heat, summer and winter, day and night, shall not cease." Genesis 8:22

This passage means that in the earth, there is always a give and take. There is always a receiving and a giving in life. So you cannot expect just to receive from somebody in multiplication if you do not know how to give it back to him or her in multiplication. When you do that, it's like you break the law. It is a universal that must take effect.

Therefore, if you don't allow the giving and receiving flow to continue, then you fragment your own life by robbing from them, or them robbing from you. In order to stay productive and prosperous, you have to allow someone to feed into you and you feed back into them. They feed into your life and you feed back into their life. If they don't feed into your life, what you do is you feed back into their life and you learn to walk away. You cannot have one person feeding life, feeding life, feeding life, and the other one is never giving life back to you. There has to be give-and-take here.

Therefore, what is happening is you are not truly prospering, if that is the case. If you are giving and not receiving back the same amount or greater of the love or the productivity or the prosperity in the sense of your attitude, their attitude, their integrity back to you, their character, their words, letting their "yes" be "yes," and their "no" be "no;" If they are not honest with you, if they are not feeding back to you that type of level of prosperity, then you are not going to prosper. You are going to stay at a place where you are going to go downhill. You will spiral downhill real quick in the level of your relationships. This will also spill over in the rest of your life and cause the rest of your life not to be prosperous. Anything in your life that is not set in the motion to prosper, it will affect other areas of your life that are prospering.

ABOVE ALL THINGS

Again, we see that 3 John 2 says, *"I wish **above all** things,"* that means everything, *"I wish above <u>all</u> things, <u>everything</u>, that you would prosper and be in health even as your soul prospers."* Which means this disciple was saying, *"I want you to prosper in spirit, soul and body. I want you to prosper in the natural just like your soul is prospering."* Which means, just as much as your soul is gaining ground, I want the natural part of you to gain ground. Because if not, then whatever area is lacking, whatever area is ignorant, (whether it be soulishly or physically), whatever area is not moving and shifting into a greater awareness of multiplication, it will effect the other arenas of your life.

Therefore, if I am prospering soulishly, but I am not prospering physically, it will spill over into my soul, and it will begin to tarnish that which is prospering. Your soul is your mind, will and emotions. Your mind governs how much knowledge and how much input you have into it… so if your mind is not receiving the prosperity of knowledge in it, then it will affect the outer part of your life, (meaning your natural/physical man).

Whatever goes in a man must come out of a man. If my soul is not prospering with the power of knowledge and wisdom, then that deficiency is going to be manifest on the outside. Once again, that is a great principle: if I am not prospering inwardly I am definitely not going to prosper outwardly. The reverse is also true: if I am not prospering outwardly, it will eventually affect my inward prosperity.

Therefore, you want to make sure that every part of your life is prospering. If there is one area of your life that is not prospering, put everything that you have into that one area to gain the knowledge, gain the wisdom, gain whatever God wants you to gain in that area to make sure it is balanced. You have to have a balance in every area of your life to make sure every area of your life is prospering.

PROSPERITY AND WHOLENESS

*But, speaking the truth in love, may grow up in all things into Him who is the head - Christ - from whom the whole body, joined and **knit together by what every joint supplies**, according to the effective working by which every part does its share, **causes growth of the body** for the edifying of itself in love. Ephesians 4:15-16*

This scripture in the Bible describes the church as a body; here it says, ***"Every joint supplies."*** This is true of your physical body, and how every organ and everything within your body supplies the need to make the entire body whole. The way that the Bible here is describing the church is that every person that makes up the church has a supply, or brings forth something to the table, that makes the whole church to function and flow the way it should; To make it whole and complete, not lacking anything.

It is the same way in your life and in your soul. Every part of it that is prospering will supply the need for your life. If one area is not supplying, it is because you have not fed into it the life it needs to cause it to have the nutrition, and value necessary, and it will cause the other areas of your life to be knocked off course or knocked off its axis. You need to watch over your life and make sure every part of you is prospering. If it is not, focus on the area that is lacking and feed life into it to ensure it will prosper and produce.

"For as the rain cometh down, and the snow from heaven, and returneth not thither, but watereth the earth, and maketh it bring forth and bud, that it may give seed to the sower, and bread to the eater: **So shall my word be** *that goeth forth out of my mouth: it shall not return unto me void, but* **it shall accomplish that which I please,** *and* **it shall prosper** *in the thing whereto I sent it." Isaiah 55:10-11*

God said something very interesting in this passage. He says He *"sends forth His word..."* That means God prophesies to us. God sends forth His word for someone to pick it up on His voice and say, *"This is what God told me for me, or this is what God told me for someone else."* As it says in Isaiah, the word that God releases into the earth cannot return back to God void. This means what God sends in the earth *as a seed form* of His voice, it has to accomplish the mission for which it was sent: For the hearer to hear what He is saying - what God has sent it to earth - for that person to hear, and begin to multiply it. You multiply the seed by believing it, by beginning to feed it, giving it attention, meditating upon it, pondering upon what God said to him. The hearer will continue to meditate on that word until he becomes that seed or that word that God sent to the earth for him or her to become in their lives. That word must "become flesh" and be an awakening, a revelation, a present reality to the one that receives it. Then it begins to prosper in what it was sent out to do in the earth within that person.

*My son, **attend** to my words; **incline thine ear** unto my*
*sayings. Let them not depart from thine eyes; **keep them***
in the midst of thine heart.
*For **they are life** unto those that find them, and health*
*to **all** their flesh. **Keep thy heart** with all diligence; for*
out of it are the issues of life. Proverbs 4:20-23

The word from God will not prosper in your life if you don't give any attention to it. If the you give no attention to it, meditate on it, nor ponder upon it then it would not be able to feed you from its life and it would not be able to produce in the area in which God sent it in. The seed of the God's word is life and health to every area of your life.

MAKE IT PROSPER

Anytime God speaks in the earth, there has to be a mind and heart to receive it because the mind is like the transmitter that says, *"I receive it or I reject it. I feed into it to make it grow or I starve it and abort it."* Therefore, God's word has to have cooperation on the earth in order for it to carry itself out. In other words, God's word has to have the mind of a person who will produce with Him as a co-creator. God is the Creator; as people made in His image, we are co-creators. In the beginning He blessed and empowered us to be fruitful, multiply and replenish the earth. (Genesis 1:28)

God wants someone who has this co-creator ability, (which is everyone on planet earth), to receive the seed and be able to multiply it, magnify it, ponder upon it, meditate upon it and make it grow. We have the power and the potential to make anything in life, body, soul and spirit, grow. We have that power from God.

Again, God says, *"I send my word forth and it cannot return back to me void,"* that means it will be taken up by someone. Someone will hear it, believe it, multiply it and begin to establish His voice in the earth for that word, or that voice to go and achieve and accomplish what it was sent to do in the earth until it manifests and becomes a reality.

The same way it is with God when He speaks, it is with us when we speak.

*So Jesus answered and said to them, "**Have faith in God**. For assuredly, I say to you, whoever says to this mountain, 'Be removed and be cast into the sea,' and does not doubt in his heart, but believes that those things he says will be done, **he will have whatever he says**."*
Mark 11:22-23
*A good man out of the good treasure of his heart bringeth forth that which is good; and an evil man out of the evil treasure of his heart bringeth forth that which is evil: **for of the abundance of the heart his mouth speaketh**. Luke 6:45*

This is why it is so important to *guard our heart with all diligence, because out of it are the issues, or the outflow of your life.* (Proverbs 4:23). When you speak out of your heart, something begins to manifest, something begins to be established and build a foundation in the reality of our lives that we can look at if nurture it and give our attention to it by what we say and think. Before long we will be able to see with our natural eye what we have seen for so long with our spiritual eye, which is our thought process and within our mind.

*Now **faith** is **the substance** of things hoped for, the*
__evidence__ of things not seen. Hebrews 11:1

Right now in my mind I can see it. I can see whatever I need in my life. Whatever I think in my life, I can see it with my eye. Before long if I think about it long enough and I see it with my mind, then what happens is, "your mind" sees it. Think about it: you think in your mind through visuals. You see colors, and you see formations, you see different things. "The mind" is what I call it life the "third eye." (Now when I say "third eye" please do not think for a moment that I am talking about some kind of new age religion, or whatever; What I am referring to as your "third eye" is the sight of your mind. It is sight that is other than natural sight. The bible says that, *"We walk by faith [supernatural substance and evidence], not by [natural] sight."* 2 Corinthians 5:7)

So when the mind sees it, before long the natural aspects of you will be able to see it the more you ponder upon it. Why? Because you are making it prosper. The more you think a thought, you are empowering it in its level of prosperity; Anything you empower, you make to prosper, whether it be healthy or harmful. Anything that you think about you are feeding and causing it to prosper. Feed those areas that are good and healthy for you in the abundance of what it needs in order for it to not only survive, but for it to explode and take off.

Setting yourself up to prosper means you have to see prosperity in every area of your life, and clean yourself out of

73

anything that doesn't match that prosperity. You have to give it your attention, mentally focus on it, you have to ponder it. Feed on abundance to the point where it is no longer just a dollar; in your mind as a thought it becomes a million dollars.

You need to learn to employ your thoughts. When you employ your thoughts, that means you have your thoughts working for you to make you more prosperous by you feeding it the nutrients it needs for it to gain ground and momentum to become prosperous.

BEARING HEALTHY FRUIT

You may be saying, "What about the natural aspect of me prospering?" Here is what you have to learn to understand; everything starts in seed form. Prosperity starts in seed form. Everything starts in the mind. Everything. No matter what it is or who you are, it starts in your thought life. You have to be able to realize that anything you desire on the outside, you have to first possess it on the inside. If not, you will never ever have it on the outside.

So many people win the lottery every year, and most people that win the lottery come from a background that it poverty-stricken, (that if you give them a hundred dollars or a thousand dollars, they think that is a lot of money), and they do not know what to do with their winnings because their mind has never prospered on that level. Because of that, what happens statistically when people win the million dollars or the lottery, they lose it within a short length of time. Within months or a year. It makes you wonder, "What on earth did they spend that money for?" Well, they did not know <u>how</u> to spend it because their mind did not prosper, and only a prosperous mind can take care of true prosperity in the natural. A mind that is poverty-stricken, or ignorant, can never truly take care of prosperity on the outside. Always remember that: prosperous minds take care of prosperous bodies. Ignorant minds can only take care of and supply the needs for ignorant bodies.

If you think about it, you cannot have one without the other. It is like the old saying, "The apple doesn't fall far from the tree," which is basically saying that the fruit is evidence to what kind of tree it is. If something is bad, no matter what you project, if you have a horrible attitude, then when you bear fruit, that fruit is going to be stinking, nasty, gross and rotten. You have to realize that it doesn't fall far from the tree.

If you look at the reality of your life, you need to realize that you cannot afford not to prosper in your mind. If you are going to have an abundance on your plate, have plenty of food, have the nice car, the nice home, whatever God desires for you as far as your business, your ministry, your talk show, whatever it is... if you are going to prosper in any of those areas, you need to first prosper mentally. If you don't, you will never get what you need in your life. <u>Ever</u>.

*This Book of the Law [**the Word of God**] shall not depart from your mouth, but you **shall meditate in it day and night**, that you may observe to do according to all that is written in it.*
*For then you will **make your way prosperous,** and then you will **have <u>good success</u>.** Have I not commanded you? Be strong and of good courage; do not be afraid, nor be dismayed, **for the Lord your God is with you wherever you go.**" Joshua 1:8-9*

This passage reiterates that what we meditate on directly effects our prosperity. The Lord told Joshua to give his full attention to God's Word, and promised that doing so would make his way prosperous, and give him good success.

You have to have an assurance, a definite confidence, about prosperity. Get _definite_ about prosperity. You have to have an assurance. _"This is definitely for me."_ That is one thing I tell people all the time, even to yourself right now you have to say, _"This prosperity is definitely for me."_ And you have to believe that with all that is in you.

If you have any old traditions, any old mindsets that make you think for a moment that money is wrong, money is bad, money is evil, you need to uproot those thoughts. The Bible never says that money is evil. It says, _"The love of money is the root of all evil." (1 Timothy 6:10)._ When you love money more than you love God, yourself and life... anytime you put money before anything, this is evil.

The reason God does not want us to love money is strictly and simply because when you put the love of money before an entity or an authority that has a voice to make a decision, then you will always be in the wrong. That means if you have a love of money that goes beyond the authority of yourself to say, "No and Yes," and build boundaries for money, if you put money first and your love is with money before those weightier things, then the money will control you, run you over and ultimately you will be destroyed.

If you put the love of money before God, you will find yourself realizing you are starving your relationship of the authority of God to say "No" in your life. To help you build those boundaries because He helped build you. He helped to build you into who you are and your identity. You are taking away from the Creator who helps the co-creator to function and flow properly. If you do that you will never succeed because you will be fragmented.

Make sure that you never put the love of money before the love of the Authority who actually creates the borders and has the voice to create the borders of where money goes, where money does not go. And learn to say "No" and learn to say "Yes" to the power of money, because money is powerful. You have to know how to control that type of money, and you make it more powerful with your mind when you begin to understand the definition of how it can work for you. If you do not know how money can work for you, then the power within money itself will control you. You become powerless because you gave the power back to money and it begins to control you and have power over you, and influences your decisions.

We see this illustrated in an encounter Jesus had with a rich, young ruler.

And when he was gone forth into the way, there came one running, and kneeled to him, and asked him, Good Master, what shall I do that I may inherit eternal life?

And Jesus said unto him, Why callest thou me good? there is none good but one, that is, God. Thou knowest the commandments, Do not commit adultery, Do not kill, Do not steal, Do not bear false witness, Defraud not, Honour thy father and mother. And he answered and said unto him, Master, all these have I observed from my youth.

Then Jesus beholding him loved him, and said unto him, One thing thou lackest: go thy way, sell whatsoever thou hast, and give to the poor, and thou shalt have treasure in heaven: and come, take up the cross, and follow me. **And he was sad at that saying, and went away grieved: for he had great possessions.**

Mark 10:17-27

This is the only account in the Bible where Jesus tells someone to sell all that he has in order to follow Him, (so it's obviously not a universal rule for everyone to obey). But Jesus loved the rich young ruler and Jesus knew that this man's love for his money was the **one thing** that was keeping him from fully following the Lord. His love for money controlled him to the point that he turned away from Jesus. Money will have power over you if you do not have power over it.

Money does have a sense of knowledge to it. It knows what it is after. But it is has no sense of boundaries. You are the one that God set over in charge, with a brain, to have control over it. You know how to control in a healthy way, because you know how to set boundaries. Money does not do that. It knows no good or bad, it has no sense of limitation or extreme, or cause and effect. It goes wherever you allow it to go. It is not designed to have control, but it will if you allow it. Money can be an out-of-control substance; therefore you have for to know how to control it.

This is the same with anything in life, like alcohol. Alcohol can bring a benefit if it is controlled. Paul instructed Timothy about the medicinal effects of wine in 1 Timothy 5:23, *"No longer drink water exclusively, but use a little wine for the sake of your stomach and your frequent ailments."* Medical studies agree that there are health benefits to drinking wine including promoting longevity, and reducing the risk of heart disease, diabetes, and stroke, just to name a few. If God approves it, hey, who are we to argue?

However, when you don't keep it controlled, you open yourself up for destruction. Alcohol has no boundaries, so when you let it take control, you will be out of control. Anything that you do not have wisdom to control by saying "No" or "Yes" to it, then that thing has the power to control you. Since it has no boundaries it will take you to the point where you ultimately die. That is how it works. Anything that has no boundaries will take you to its limits until there is no more left of who you are because you do not have an identity, unless you take it back.

So, always be in control. Always be in control. Use your authority wisely over substances, over things, over anything that God has created because you are called to be the master of it and not the servant of anything. The only thing you are called to serve is God. Other than that, everything else you are the master and the lord over. You are going to have to learn to know how to discipline, how to say "No," and how to say, "Yes." That only comes from a prosperous mind.

When you build boundaries you are on the road to a prosperous life. When you know how to say "No," you are on the road to a prosperous life. When you know how to formulate thoughts in your brain that God wants you to have, you are on the way to a prosperous life. Anytime you remove the junk and fill your mind full of treasure, of good teachings, good valuable things, walking in maturity, then you are on your way to prospering.

WRITE THE VISION

One of the things you should also do is write down your desires. If you are setting yourself up to prosper, write down your desires. Write down on a piece of paper exactly what you are looking for. Be specific.

I tell people all the time, God doesn't want you to sit here being indecisive and find your saying, "Well, I think I will just... uh.. yeah that sounds good. Everyone else has one, so I will take that too." No, God wants you to be specific.

God uses the universe, creation, and things in life to prosper you. And yet some people might say, "Uh, I don't believe that. God is the one that does it." Then let me ask you a question, why did God say in the Bible that He would prosper you? The Bible promises that God would give you favor with God and man, (Proverbs 3:4). He also says that he will cause man to give into your bosom, (Luke 6:38). Another word for "favor" is "prosperity." So, God uses man to prosper you as well. Not only does God favor you and give you prosperity, and not only does He want you to be a co-creator to be able to gain ground, create your day and gain prosperity, but He also will use mortal man to favor you and give you prosperity.

So God does use creation. In the Numbers 22:28, God even used a donkey to prophecy to his master. God can and will use His creation to get His point across to whoever is listening, whoever has an ear to hear and an eye to see. God will use anything and everything He can in creation to get His point across to you of what He wants you to have, and He will use creation to push it in your direction and give you the desires of your heart.

*And we know that **all things work together for good** to them that love God, to them who are the called according to his purpose.*
Romans 8:28

*Delight yourself in the Lord; and **He will give you the desires of your heart.** Psalm 37:4*

Proverbs 13:22 even says, *"The wealth of the wicked is laid up for the righteous."* Wicked in this context are those who do wrong in the sight of God in the sense of being fragmented, not knowing the integrity, not knowing that they are whole, not knowing the righteousness, peace, and joy in the Holy Spirit, not knowing the power of giving, not knowing how to use their thoughts properly, not knowing how to feed their life with nutritious valuable things. Because of that, their wealth is transferred or laid-up for those who know how to handle money, for those who know their God, and those who know how to treat the things of God that He has placed in the earth by giving it value, respect, honor, multiplication and the understanding of knowing how to make it work for the good of humanity.

You have the wealth of the wicked. Even the wicked will give you wealth. It is not just about God giving it to you, it is about His creation giving it to you, it is about man giving it to you, and even the wicked. The wicked are set up as servants to even bless you.

You have to realize that God will supply what you need.

As a man thinketh in his heart, so is he.
Proverbs 23:7

Beloved, I wish above all things that you would prosper,
*and be in health **even as your soul prospers**. 3 John 2*

In order to prosper naturally, you have to prosper mentally. In order to prosper mentally, you have to prosper spiritually. In order to get what you need in the natural, as far as the material things that you are looking for that you know God has promised you, (you know that you desperately need a new car, you desperately need a new home because you have three children now and at first you had one child, or the money aspect of it, or a new job), any of that stuff all comes from an internal realm of prosperity. When you learn how to prosper internally, then externally you will prosper in any and every area of your life.

Write down your desire of your heart. That is your foundation: those things that you know that you know that you know that you need for your life. "This is what I need. This is what I must have for me. Not because somebody else has it, but because this is what I need in order for my life to be where it needs to be in the kingdom of heaven."

WHY SETTLE FOR LITTLE...

There is a principle that I want you to begin to remember. That is: Why settle for little, when you can have so much more? **Again,** Why settle for little, when you can have so much more? In order to get prosperity on the outside you are going to have to prosper mentally. Mentally means you can no longer look in the small areas of your life. It is not about something small, not about the little things. Because bottom line is, you have to remember, it is the big things. If you need the big items, you need the big amounts of money. If you need large things, you need the large things that know how to purchase it. Therefore, why think small when you can think big? Why think a hundred dollars when you can think a thousand or a million dollars.

Why think a million when you can think a billion. Why think small when you can focus on something that is out of your reach? The main thing you want to do is do not focus on something that is within your reach now. If you say, "I am meditating by the law of attraction by God that I am going to have a thousand dollars next week," and yet your paycheck might be the thousand dollars. You have to be able to think outside the box to something that you normally would not be able to get your hands on. That makes it a miracle.

When you reach outside the box of something that naturally you know you could not get your hands on, it sets God up to bring a miracle. Therefore, it only comes packaged by the miraculous and not something that just happened because it is what you normally get anyway, or is in the reach of your hands to get it anyway.

You have to realize, why settle for little when you can shoot for the stars for much bigger things than what you normally have.

When you focus on the stars and focus on the unlimited part of things you normally would not have that you can get your hands on, and then you will begin to set your standards higher. You begin to cause your mind to grow with the universe at a greater expansion than you have ever done before because you are stepping outside the box. You have realized, "I don't want to be spiritually middle-class. I don't want to be spiritually bottom of the totem pole. I want to be prosperous. I want to be in the high-class. I want to be among the higher echelon. I want to be among the rich." In order to do that you are going to have to think it, believe it, and than you become it. You are going to have to look at everything in your life to make sure, "Is this something that I need, that is a display or a reflection to me back of something that is prosperous?"

Let me give you a great example. When you deal with cars, you can look at the true level of prosperity does not always say, "I have to have a Jaguar. I have to have a Mercedes." A true level of prosperity could mean for you, "Hey, I want a brand new Honda because Hondas will hold their value. They are great cars. Ergonomically, they are amazing, plus they hold their value. They don't break down quite as easy. You can keep them longer, and when you sell it you can get more money for it than you can a Jaguar. When you need help or something breaks down on it, it won't cost you thousands upon thousands of dollars. It won't cost you that much to work on."

You have to think, what is true prosperity in that level. For many people, such as myself years ago, I had Hondas for a number of years because that was the true realm or level of prosperity for me during that time. It was not about how much to spend, but about the wisdom behind the prosperity that in the long run I get more back for my car because it holds its value when I turn around and sell it. More so than a Jaguar would give that I spent a lot of money on. With a Honda, it becomes a level of a win-win situation because I moved out of the mind of wisdom. That is what you call true prosperity. Do not settle for little when you can settle for much more.

Do not settle for little when your mind can be able to shoot for the stars, and ask God for more. You can only ask God for more when your mind and your soul is prospering. When your mind is prospering, then and only then, will its appetite change and say, "I am hungry for something more. I am not hungry anymore for candy bars. I am now hungry for steak. I am hungry for lobster. I am hungry for caviar. I am hungry for something that has more of a valuable substance because my needs have shifted, and that is what my nutrition needs now. I have shifted to that nutrition. I need the protein." Your mind will then begin to shift what it needs to a higher place.

That higher place is no longer going to be just candy bars. I am talking spiritually. Your thoughts will begin to transform to something that now requires other higher valuable nutritious things to sustain it. It's the same way in the natural. Do not settle for something small, "empty calories." When you reach towards the stars, your nutritional, substance, mineral and protein needs will change and you will require more that will allow you to prosper at a higher level mentally. That is the main thing you want to be able to do within your life.

PROSPEROUS WORDS

Prosperous thinking will lead to prosperous will lead to prosperous speaking.

*For of the abundance of the heart **his mouth speaketh**.*
Luke 6:45

Death and life are in the power of the tongue: and they
that love it shall eat the fruit thereof.
Proverbs 18:21

Speak daily affirmations to yourself. Speak words of life over yourself all day long. Speak life over yourself. Speak life to your house, your car, your money, and your job. Speak life to everything. Make positive affirmations. I like to call them proclamations or declarations. Make strong, positive, prosperous statements.

If you talk gutter language, you are talking poverty. I am not talking about being fake. I am not talking about making sure you speak eloquent words that you yourself barely know the definitions to, which have nothing to do with speaking prosperous. It means speaking things that _have value_ when you speak them.

When people speak, have you ever found that you sometimes tune them out? Maybe because what they are saying just does not seem that important? Often it is because they are not speaking of prosperous things. They are speaking of things that are coming out of their soulish man, or what I call their consciousness of just speaking. *"I am talking just to talk."*

Alternatively, many other people speak in a way where you know that they know what they are saying because they have lived it, they have experienced it, and they are speaking valuable insights into the conversation. What happens is, that conversation becomes powerful and prosperous and people want to pay attention. They say, "Oh, go back and tell me that again. What was that you just said? That's powerful. That's good. I can apply that to my life." Then they are not only thinking prosperous, they are also speaking prosperous, and that refreshes those who hear them.

The words of a man's mouth are as deep waters, and the wellspring of wisdom as a flowing brook. Proverbs 18:4

You always want to speak prosperous and positive affirmations out of your mouth. You need to train your mouth, your mind, your body, your soul, your spirit, and your lifestyle to think prosperous on every level.

Prosperity basically means "an abundance of; and overwhelming sense of substance." You can't look at your life and just say, "It is void here, it's void there, but I am still prospering." Nope, you will not prosper. Fill your life full of substance, of value, of integrity, of a higher echelon mentality even when you speak. Therefore what you speak you will have, and what you think you will become. In every part of your life will be prosperous. That is how you set yourself up to prosper. Once you get this going in your life, it becomes a win-win situation. Everything in your life from that moment on will ultimately prosper in your life.

BIO OF DR. JEREMY LOPEZ:

Dr. Jeremy Lopez is Founder and President of **Identity Network International, Sounds for Now, Awakening to Your Now** and **Now is Your Moment.** Identity Network is a prophetic resource website that reaches well over 153,000 people around the globe and distributes books and teaching CD's. Jeremy has taught and prophesied to thousands of people from all walks of life such as local church congregations, producers, investors, business owners, attorneys, city leaders, musicians, and various ministries around the world concerning areas such as finding missing children, financial breakthroughs, parenthood, and life changing decisions.

Dr. Jeremy Lopez is an international teacher and motivational speaker. Dr. Jeremy speaks on new dimensions of revelatory knowledge in scripture, universal laws, mysteries, patterns, and cycles. He has a love for all people and desires to enrich their lives with love, grace and the mercy of God and to empower them to be successful. Dr. Jeremy believes it is time to awake the Christ Conscious mind and live out the victorious life that was meant for us. His desire is to live a life filled with purpose, potential, and destiny. He ministers with a revelational prophetic teaching gift that brings a freshness of the word of the Lord to people everywhere.

This is accomplished through conferences, prophetic meetings, and seminars. He serves on many governing boards, speaks to business leaders across the nation, and also holds a Doctorate of Divinity. He has had the privilege of ministering prophetically to Governor Bob Riley of Alabama. He has also ministered to thousands overseas including millionaires around the world. He has traveled to many nations including Jamaica, Prague, Paris, Indonesia, Haiti, Hong Kong, Taiwan, UK, Mexico, Singapore, Bahamas, Costa Rica, Puerto Rico, etc. He has hosted and been a guest on several radio and TV programs from Indonesia to New York.

He is the author of nationally published books, 'The Laws of Financial Progression,' 'The Power of the Eternal Now' *(Destiny Image)* and his newest book, 'Releasing the Power of the Prophetic' *(Chosen Books)*. He has also recorded over 45 teaching CD's.

Jeremy's ministry has been recognized by many national leaders and other prophetic leaders around the nation.

For more information on Dr. Jeremy Lopez, please visit www.DrJeremyLopez.com.

Dr. Jeremy Lopez has many books, e-books, audio downloads, and teaching CDs for you to enjoy and to grow.

OTHER PRODUCT BY DR. LOPEZ:

Books:

Abandoned To Divine Destiny:
You Were Before Time (book)
by Jeremy Lopez

The Power of the Eternal Now (book)
by Jeremy Lopez

The Laws of Financial Progression (book)
by Dr. Jeremy Lopez

Releasing the Power of the Prophetic:
A Practical Guide to Developing a Listening Ear and
Discerning Spirit (book)
by Jeremy Lopez

41992226R00055

Made in the USA
Middletown, DE
14 April 2019